CARLSBAD CAVERNS
NATIONAL PARK
ACTIVITY BOOK

PUZZLES, MAZES, GAMES, AND MORE ABOUT
CARLSBAD CAVERNS NATIONAL PARK

NATIONAL PARKS ACTIVITIES SERIES

CARLSBAD CAVERNS NATIONAL PARK ACTIVITY BOOK

Copyright 2022
Published by Little Bison Press

The author acknowledges that the land on which Carlsbad Caverns National Park is located are the traditional lands of the Ndé Kónitsąąíí Gokíyaa (Lipan Apache) and Mescalero Apache Tribes.

LITTLE BISON
Press

For more free national parks activities, visit
www.littlebisonpress.com

About Carlsbad Caverns National Park

Carlsbad Caverns National Park is located in the Guadalupe Mountains in the state of New Mexico. The park is just a few miles from the city of Carlsbad, New Mexico.

Secretly tucked below the desert terrain, this park is famous for having more than 119 caves, formed when sulfuric acid dissolved limestone, leaving behind caverns big and small. Above the ground in the Chihuahuan Desert are ancient sea ledges, rocky canyons, cacti, grasses, and desert wildlife that will capture your attention.

Visitors will find opportunities for hiking, backcountry camping, and horseback riding. From late May to October, visitors can attend a ranger-led talk about bats before their evening flight. From the Bat Flight Amphitheater, visitors can witness thousands of Brazilian free-tailed bats emerge from Carlsbad Cavern in search of food.

Carlsbad Caverns National Park is famous for:
- 119 caves
- Hiking, backcountry camping, and horseback riding
- Bat Flight Program

Hey, I'm Parker!

I'm the only snail in history to visit every National Park in the United States! Come join me on my adventures in Carlsbad Caverns National Park.

Throughout this book, we will learn about the history of the park, the animals and plants that live here, and things to do if you ever visit in person. This book is also full of games and activities!

Last but not least, I am hidden 9 times on different pages. See how many times you can find me. This page doesn't count!

Carlsbad Caverns Bingo

Let's play bingo! Cross off each box you are able to during your visit to the national park. Try to get a bingo down, across, or diagonally. If you can't visit the park, use the bingo board to plan your perfect trip.

Pick out some activities you would want to do during your visit. What would you do first? How long would you spend there? What animals would you try to see?

SPOT A LIZARD	TOUR THE CAVES	GO FOR A HIKE	TAKE A PICTURE AT AN OVERLOOK	WATCH A MOVIE AT THE VISITORS CENTER
IDENTIFY A TREE	LEARN ABOUT THE INDIGENOUS PEOPLE WHO LIVE IN THIS AREA	WITNESS A SUNRISE OR SUNSET	OBSERVE THE NIGHT SKIES	ATTEND THE BAT FLIGHT PROGRAM
HEAR A BIRD CALL	TAKE A STAR WALK	FREE SPACE	LEARN ABOUT THE IMPORTANCE OF THE BATS	SPOT SOME ANIMAL TRACKS
PICK UP TEN PIECES OF TRASH	HAVE A PICNIC	SEE A MULE DEER	HIKE IN THE CHIHUAHUAN DESERT	SPOT A BIRD OF PREY
LEARN ABOUT THE GEOLOGY OF THE CAVERNS	SEE SOMEONE RIDING A HORSE	GO CAMPING	VISIT A RANGER STATION	LEARN ABOUT WHITE-NOSE SYNDROME

Protecting the Park

When you visit national parks, it is important to leave the park the way you found it. Did you know that the national parks get hundreds of millions of visitors every year? We can only protect national parks for future visitors to enjoy if everyone does their part. The choices we make when visiting the park have a big impact.

Read each line below. Write a sentence or draw a picture to show the impacts these changes would make on the park.

What would happen if every visitor fed the wild animals?

What would happen if every visitor picked a flower?

What would happen if every visitor took home a few rocks?

What would happen if every visitor wrote or carved their name into a cave wall?

Park Poetry

America's parks inspire art of all kinds. Painters, sculptors, photographers, writers, and artists of all mediums have taken inspiration from natural beauty. They have turned their inspiration into great works.

Use this space to write your own poem about the park. Think about what you have experienced or seen. Use descriptive language to create an acrostic poem. This type of poem has the first letter of each line spell out another word. Create an acrostic that spells out the word "Cavern."

C _____

A _____

V _____

E _____

R _____

N _____

C ave bats

A viate across

V ast skies

E xploring

R avishing

N ew Mexico

C rickets chirp

A cross the desert

V iews

E ager for sunrise

R eady to explore

N ew places

Color Carlsbad Cavern

Carlsbad Caverns is just one of over 119 caves in the national park with the same name. It is one of the few caves open to the public.

Go Horseback Riding on the Guadalupe Ridge Trail

Help find the horse's lost shoe!

start here →

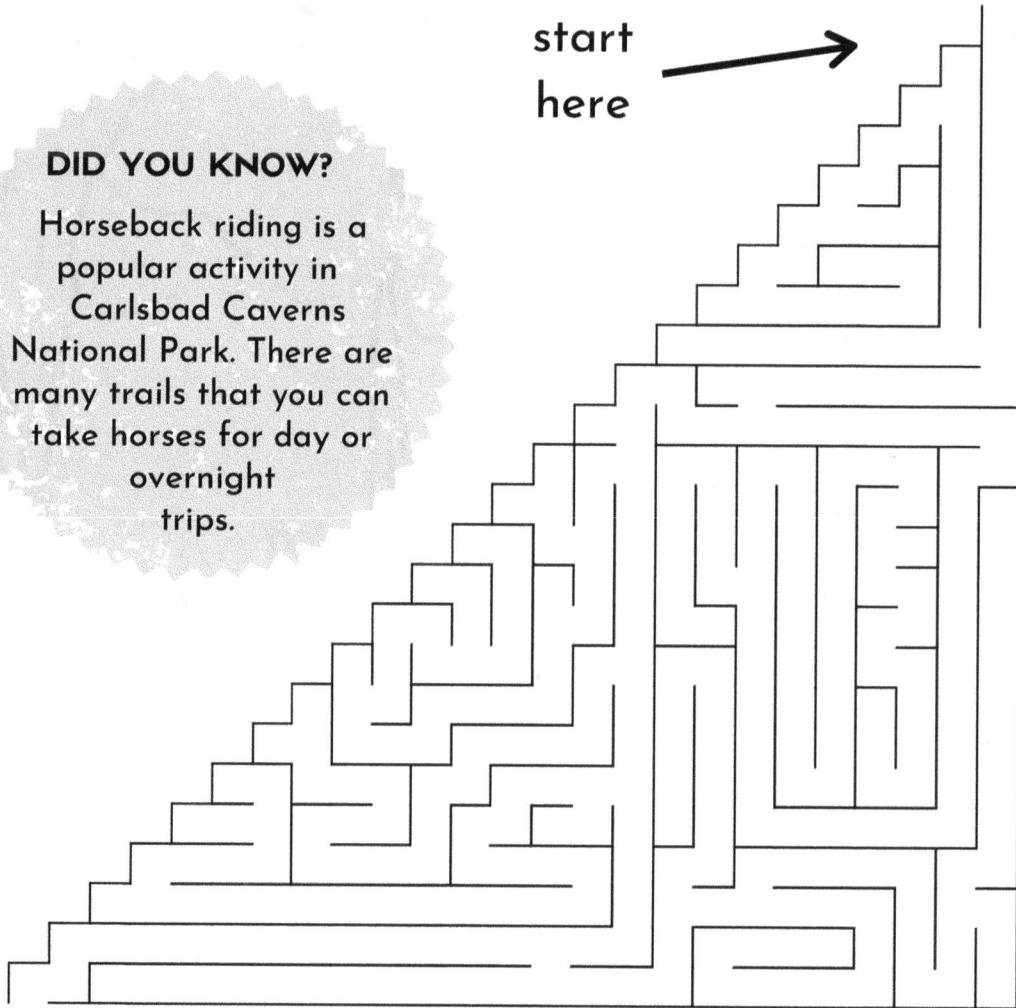

Camping Packing List

What should you take with you when you go camping? Pretend you are in charge of your family camping trip. Make a list of what you would need to be safe and comfortable on an overnight excursion. Some considerations are listed on the side.

1.
2.
3.
4.
5.
6.
7.
8.
9.
10.
11.
12.
13.
14.
15.
16.

- What will you eat at every meal?

- What will the weather be like?

- Where will you sleep?

- What will you do during your free time?

- How luxurious do you want camp to be?

- How will you cook?

- How will you see at night?

- How will you dispose of trash?

- What might you need in case of emergencies?

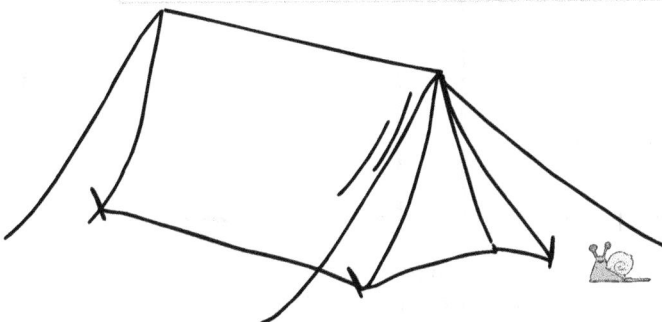

While there aren't any developed campgrounds in Carlsbad Caverns NP, there are plenty of spots in the surrounding Bureau of Land Management areas where you can set up camp!

Carlsbad Caverns National Park

Date: _____

Season: _____

Who I went with: _____

Which entrance: _____

How was your experience? Write a few sentences about your trip. Where did you stay? What did you do? What was your favorite activity? If you haven't visited the park yet, write a paragraph pretending that you did.

_____

_____

_____

_____

_____

_____

STAMPS

Many national parks and monuments have cancellation stamps for visitors to use. These rubber stamps record the date and location that you visited. Many people collect the markings as a free souvenir. Check with a ranger to see where you can find a stamp during your visit. If you aren't able to find one, you can draw your own.

Where is the Park?

Carlsbad Caverns National Park is in the southwestern United States, in the state of New Mexico. Nicknamed the Land of Enchantment, New Mexico shares a border with the country Mexico.

New Mexico

Look at the shape of New Mexico. Can you find it on the map? If you are from the US, can you find your home state? Color New Mexico red. Put a star on the map where you live.

Connect the Dots #1

Connect the dots to figure out what this tiny critter is. There are ten types of these that live in Carlsbad Caverns National Park.

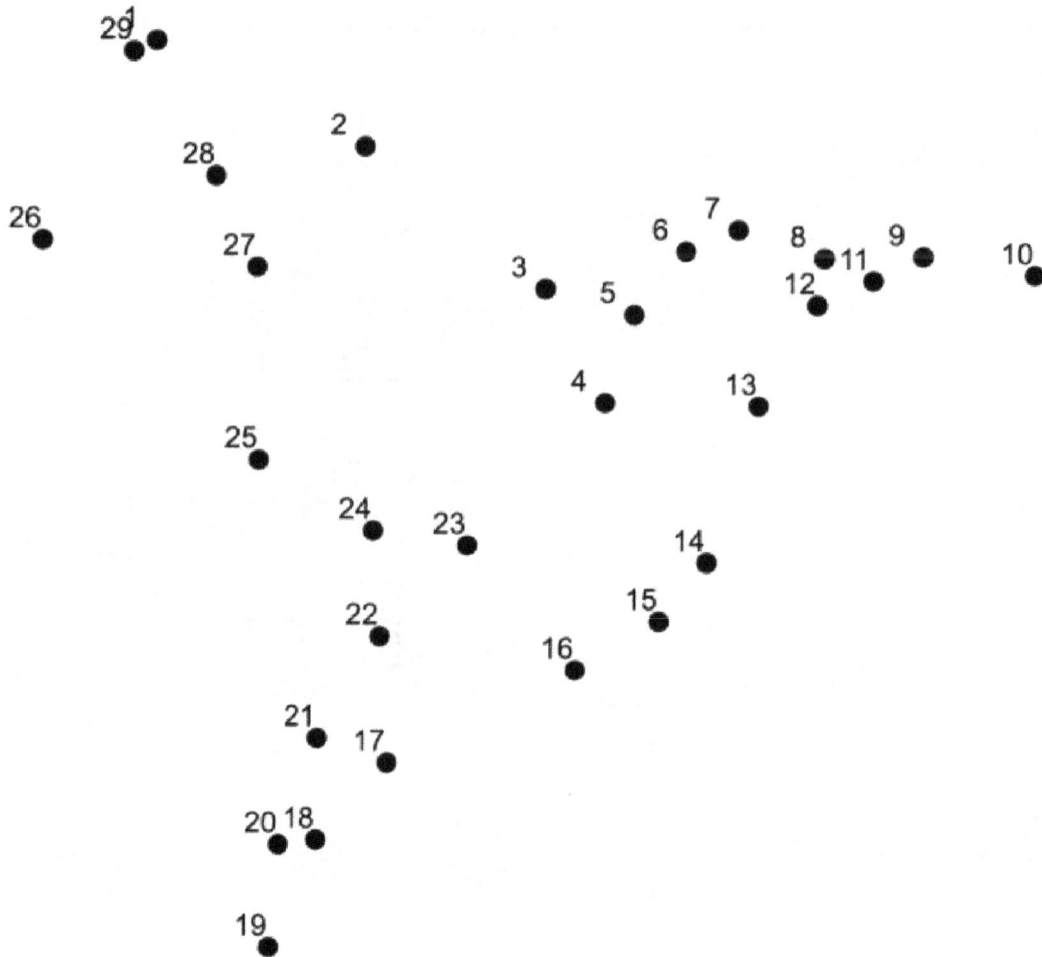

1
29
2
28
26
27
7
6
8 11 9
3
5 12 10
4 13
25
24 23
14
22 15
16
21 17
20 18
19

Their heart rate can reach as high as 1,260 beats per minute and a breathing rate of 250 breaths per minute. Have you ever measured your breathing rate? Ask a friend or family member to set a timer for 60 seconds. Once they say "go," try to breathe normally. Count each breath until they say "stop." How do your breaths per minute compare to hummingbirds?

_____

_____

The Western Pipistrelle is the smallest bat in the United States. They often come out during the daytime and can be seen flying about in the afternoon, catching flying insects.

Badgers eat a variety of burrowing animals. They are mostly nocturnal, but can occasionally be seen during the day.

Who lives here?

Below are 8 plants and animals that live in the park.
Use the word bank to fill in the clues below.

WORD BANK: BADGER, BUFFALOBUR, WILLET, YUMA MYOTIS, RACCOON, SPARROW, PIPISTRELLE, TEXAS TOAD

☐☐☐ C ☐☐☐

☐☐☐ A ■☐☐☐☐☐☐

☐☐☐☐ R ☐☐

☐☐☐ L ☐☐

☐☐☐☐ S ☐☐☐☐☐☐

☐☐☐☐☐☐☐ B ☐☐

☐☐☐ A ☐■☐☐☐☐

☐☐ D ☐☐☐

Texas Toads can go dormant in the hottest months of the year by burying themselves in mud or cooler soils until conditions become favorable again.

The Black-throated Sparrow is commonly seen near the cave entrance area year-round.

Common Names
vs.
Scientific Names

A common name of an organism is a name that is based on everyday language. You have heard the common names of plants, animals, and other living things on tv, in books, and at school. Common names can also be referred to as "English" names, popular names, or farmer's names. Common names can vary from place to place. The word for a particular tree may be one thing, but that same tree has a different name in another country. Common names can even vary from region to region, even in the same country.

Scientific names, or Latin names, are given to organisms to make it possible to have uniform names for the same species. Scientific names are in Latin. You may have heard plants or animals referred to by their scientific name or parts of their scientific names. Latin names are also called "binomial nomenclature," which refers to a two-part naming system. The first part of the name – the generic name – refers to the genus to which the species belongs. The second part of the name, the specific name, identifies the species. For example, Tyrannosaurus rex is an example of a widely known scientific name.

American Black Bear

Ursus americanus

COMMON NAME

Elk

Cervus canadensis

LATIN NAME = GENUS + SPECIES

Elk = Cervus canadensis

Black Bear = Ursus americanus

Find the Match!
Common Names and Latin Names

Match the common name to the scientific name for each animal. The first one is done for you. Use clues on the page before and after this one to complete the matches.

Elk	Aquila chrysaetos
Western Water Hemlock	Ursus americanus
Torrey Yucca	Actitis macularius
American Black Bear	Lampropeltis getula
Great Horned Owl	Cicuta douglasii
Golden Eagle	Myotis velifer
Spotted Sandpiper	Bubo virginianus
Desert Kingsnake	Cervus canadensis
Cave Myotis	Yucca torreyi

Golden Eagle

Aquila chrysaetos

Spotted Sandpiper
Actitis macularius

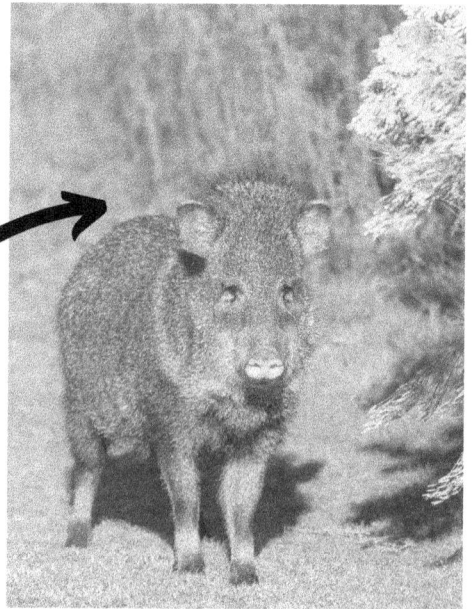

Collard Peccary or Javelina
Pecari tajacu

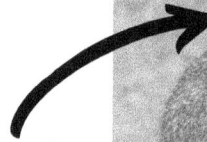

Great Horned Owl
Bubo virginianus

Some plants and animals that live at Carlsbad Caverns

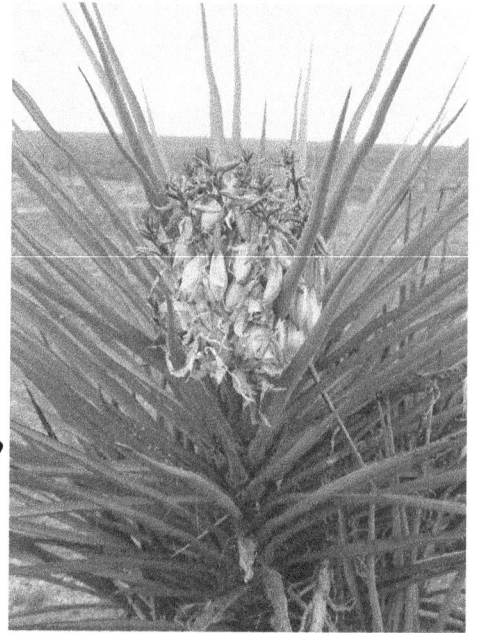

Torrey Yucca
Yucca torreyi

Cave Myotis
Myotis velifer

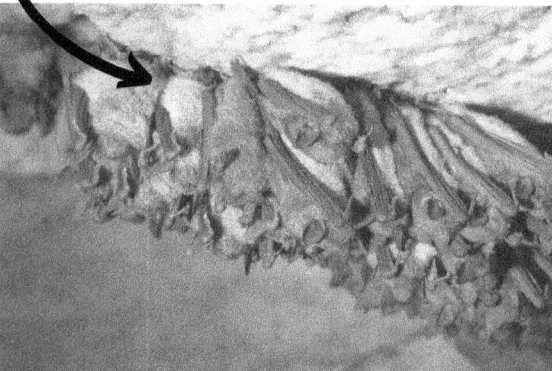

Desert Kingsnake
Lampropeltis getula

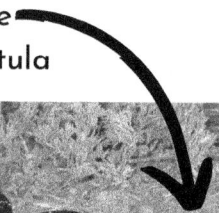

Things To Do Jumble

Unscramble the letters to uncover activities you can do while in Carlsbad Caverns National Park. Hint: each one ends in -ing.

1. SARTGZA ☐☐☐☐☐☐☐☐☐ING

2. HKI ☐☐☐ING

3. RIDB ☐☐☐☐ING

4. MACP ☐☐☐☐ING

5. KINICPC ☐☐☐☐☐☐☐ING

6. EISSTEHG ☐☐☐☐☐☐☐☐ING

7. VACE LOEPRX ☐☐☐☐■■☐☐☐☐☐ING

Word Bank

birding
reading
camping
stargazing
horseback riding
hiking
hunting
singing
cave exploring
sightseeing
picnicking

Making a Difference

It is important to protect the valuable resources of the world, not only beautiful places like national parks.

How many of these things do you do at home? If you answered "no" to more than 10 items, talk to the grown-ups in your life to see if there are any household habits you might be able to change. Conserving our collective resources helps us all.

Yes	No	Do you...
☐	☐	turn off the water when you are brushing your teeth?
☐	☐	use LED light bulbs when possible?
☐	☐	use a reusable water bottle instead of disposable ones?
☐	☐	ride your bike or take the bus instead of riding in the car?
☐	☐	have a rain barrel under your roof gutters to collect rain water?
☐	☐	take quick showers?
☐	☐	avoid putting more food on your plate than you will eat?
☐	☐	take reusable lunch containers?
☐	☐	grow a garden?
☐	☐	buy items with less packaging?
☐	☐	recycle paper?
☐	☐	recycle plastic?
☐	☐	have a compost pile at home so you can make your own soil?
☐	☐	pick up trash when you see it on the trail?
☐	☐	plan a "staycation" and fly only when you have to?

____ ____
of   # of
Yes   No

Add up your score! Are there any "no"s that you want to turn into a yes?

Can you think of any other ways to protect our natural resources?

_____

Helping Bats Thrive

Bats in North America are under threat of a disease called white-nose syndrome. What is this disease? How does it affect bats? What can you do to help?

White-nose syndrome is caused by a fungus called *Pseudogymnoascus destructans*, or *Pd* for short. It affects cave-dwelling bats. Unfortunately, this disease is fatal and has killed millions of bats across the United States and Canada. A symptom of this disease is right in the name - a white fuzzy patch on a bat's nose and face. The disease also causes bats to act strangely; they will fly outside in winter when they should be hibernating.

The fungus *Pd* can be spread from bat to bat, but it can also be spread when bats touch cave surfaces with the fungus. Humans are potential carriers, which is why decontamination is important when visiting the caves at Carlsbad Caverns National Park.

Bats play an important role in our ecosystem. They help control insect populations. Reducing the spread of white-nose syndrome supports bats and their survival.

What can you do to help stop the spread of white-nose syndrome?

```
__  L  __  __  __       Y  __  __  __  __     __  __  __  __  __ ,
1      +   @   ^             =  5   ?         $  2   =   +   $

__  L  __  __  __  __  __ ,  __  __  __     __  __  __  __
1      =   %  2   +   $       @   ^   &       ¿   +   @   ?

 B  __  __  __  __  __     __  __  __     __  __  __  __  __
    +   *   =   ?   +       @   ^   &      @   *   %   +   ?

__  __  __  __  __     __  __  __  __     @  __     Y  __  __  __
¿   =   !   ^   ¿      !   ^   %   =         ^      1  @   <   +
```

a	c	d	e	f	g	h	i	n	o	p	r	s	t	u	v
@	1	&	+	*	¿	2	!	^	=	4	?	$	%	5	<

21

The National Park Logo

The National Park System has over 400 units in the US. Just like Carlsbad Caverns National Park, each location is unique or special in some way. The areas include other national parks, historic sites, monuments, seashores, and other recreation areas.

Each element of the National Park emblem represents something that the National Park Service protects. Fill in each blank below to show what each symbol represents.

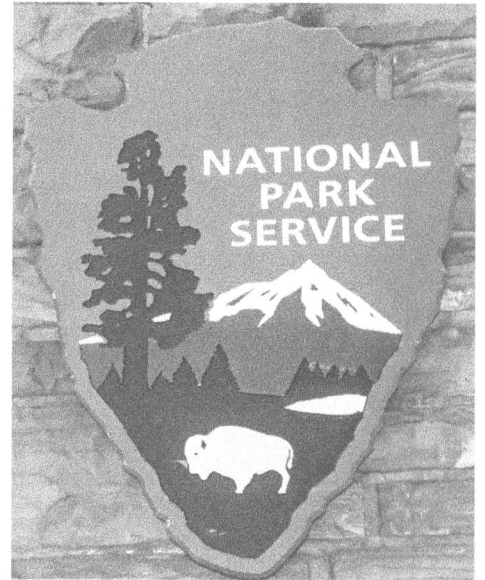

```
WORD BANK:
MOUNTAINS, ARROWHEAD, BISON,
SEQUOIA TREE, WATER
```

This represents all plants: _____

This represents all animals: _____

This represents the landscapes: _____

This represents the waters protected by the park service: _____

This represents the historical and archeological values: _____

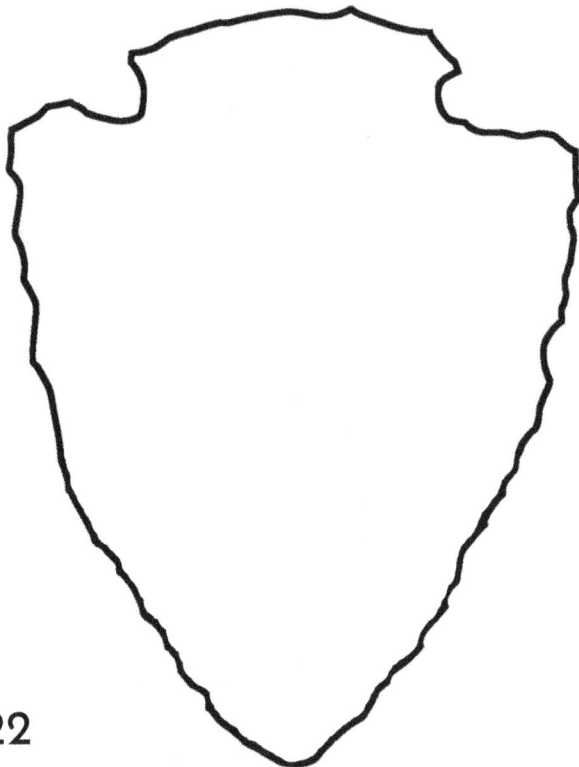

Now it's your turn! Pretend you are designing a new national park. Add elements to the design that represent the things your park protects.

What is the name of your park?

Describe why you included the symbols that you included. What do they mean?

The Ten Essentials

Careful preparation and knowledge are key to a successful adventure into Carlsbad Cavern's backcountry.

The ten essentials are a list of things that are important to have when you go for longer hikes. If you go on a hike to the <u>backcountry</u>, it is especially important that you have everything you need in case of an emergency. If you get lost or something unforeseen happens, it is good to be prepared to survive until help finds you.

The ten essentials list was developed in the 1930s by an outdoors group called the Mountaineers. Over time and technological advancements, this list has evolved. Can you identify all the things on the current list? Circle each of the "essentials" and cross out everything that doesn't make the cut.

fire: matches, lighter, tinder, and/or stove	a pint of milk	extra money	headlamp, plus extra batteries	extra clothes
extra water	a dog	Polaroid camera	bug net	lightweight games, such as a deck of cards
extra food	a roll of duct tape	shelter	sun protection such as sunglasses, sun-protective clothes and sunscreen	knife, plus a gear repair kit
a mirror	navigation: map, compass, altimeter, GPS device, or satellite messenger	first aid kit	extra flip-flops	entertainment such as video games or books

Backcountry - a remote undeveloped rural area.

Connect the Dots #2

This animal lives in almost every state in the US, including Carlsbad Caverns National Park. They are nocturnal, more active at night, and sleep during the day. They are omnivorous eaters, which means they eat both plants and animals.

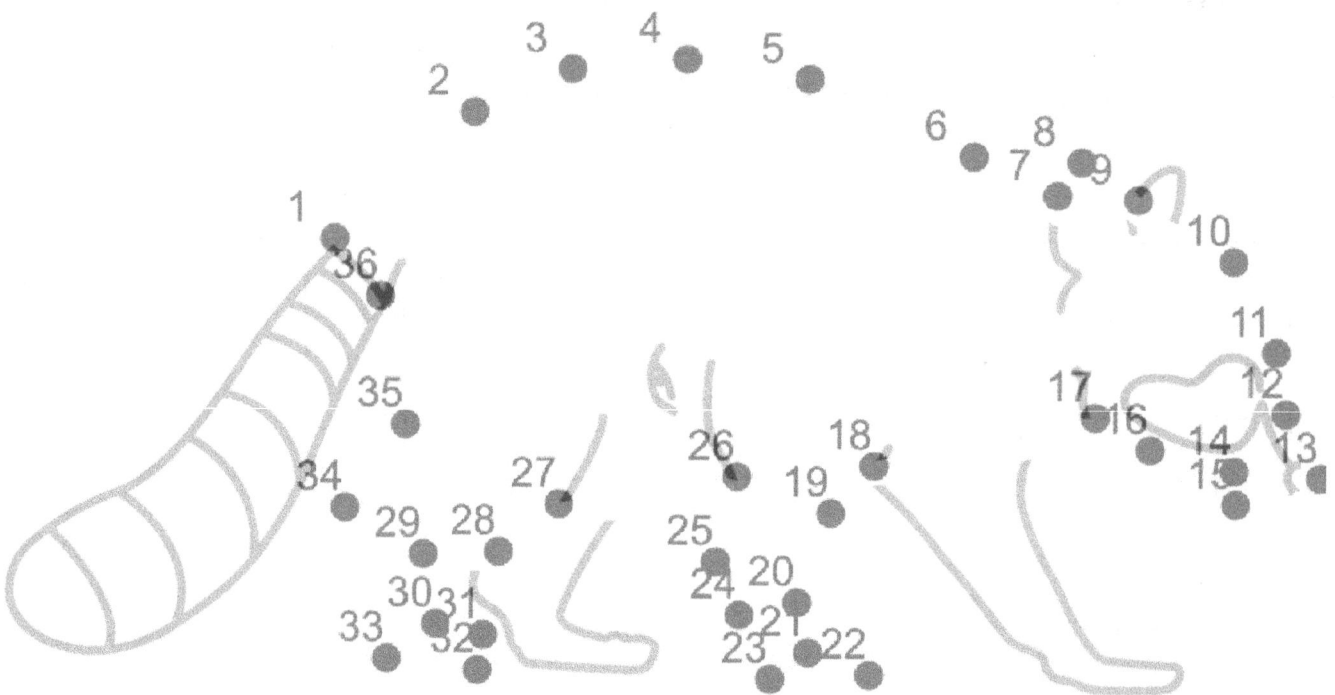

Are you an omnivore like a raccoon? An herbivore only eats plant foods. A carnivore only eats meat. An omnivore eats both. What type of eater are you? Write down some of your favorite foods to back up your answer.

_____

_____

Carlsbad Caverns Word Search

Words may be horizontal, vertical, diagonal,
or they might even be backwards!

1. caves
2. bat
3. elevator
4. New Mexico
5. balloon ballroom
6. guano
7. cave swallow
8. bat cave
9. deer
10. stalagmite
11. flowstone
12. lily pads
13. popcorn
14. draperies
15. Pinchot
16. Lechuguilla
17. sotol
18. Jim White
19. mining
20. Guadalupe

```
B A L L O O N B A L L R O O M
H A A S K I L O C E E L D N J
T E T R A A O S C C A V E S B
S M I N I N G S C H R L E C C
T E A D I A B L O U I U R A L
A O L D T O N A U G T E A S I
L E E P U L A D A U G R I C N
A L B A M O I E P I N C H O T
G E P R O T A V E L E D Y D E
M C O C C O O Y H L W G J E N
I T P H C S I N O A M E I S O
T R C I K O E I S B E K M R T
E I O S H Z I R A I X A W G S
J C R O L O V T S O C R H E W
N I N A K M C N E R O L I E O
L I L Y P A D S L Z E S T N L
H Y D R V D R A P E R I E S F
C A V E S W A L L O W A L A M
```

Jim White was a young cowboy who is credited with being one of the earliest
known people who explored the caves in depth. To learn more about Jim's
story, make sure to tour Carlsbad Cavern.

25

Wildlife Wisdom

The national park is home to many different kinds of animals. Seeing wildlife can be an exciting part of visiting the national park but it is important to remember that these animals are wild. They need plenty of space and a healthy habitat where they can find their own food. Part of this is not allowing animals to eat any human food. This is their home and we are the visitors. We need to be respectful of the wildlife in the park.

Directions: Circle the highlighted words that best complete the following sentences.

If an animal changes its behavior because of your presence, you are:
   A) too close
   B) funny looking
   C) dehydrated and should drink more water

The best thing we can do to help wild animals survive is:
   A) make them pets
   B) protect their habitat
   C) knit them winter sweaters

In a national park, it is okay to share your food with wild animals:
   A) never
   B) always
   C) sometimes

When you're hiking in an area where there are bears, you should warn bears that you are entering their space by:
   A) hiking quietly
   B) making noise
   C) wearing bright colors

At night, park rangers care for the animals by:
   A) putting them back into their cages
   B) tucking them into bed
   C) leaving them alone

If you see an abandoned bird's nest, it is best to:
   A) pet the baby birds
   B) leave it alone
   C) crunch the empty eggshells

Bears look under logs in hopes of finding:
   A) granola bars
   B) insects
   C) peanuts to eat

The place where an animal lives is called its:
   A) condo
   B) habitat
   C) crib

Snail Mail

Design a postcard to send to a friend or family member. Who do you want to tell about Carlsbad Caverns National Park? In the first template, write your message. In the second template, create a design for the front of the postcard. You could show something you saw, something you did, or something you want to do in the national park.

Postcard

The Perfect Picnic Spot

Fill in the blanks on this page without looking at the full story. Once you have each line filled out, use the words you've chosen to complete the story on the next page.

EMOTION _____

FOOD _____

SOMETHING SWEET _____

STORE _____

MODE OF TRANSPORTATION _____

NOUN _____

SOMETHING ALIVE _____

SAUCE _____

PLURAL VEGETABLES _____

ADJECTIVE _____

PLURAL BODY PART _____

ANIMAL _____

PLURAL FRUIT _____

PLACE _____

SOMETHING TALL _____

COLOR _____

ADJECTIVE _____

NOUN _____

A DIFFERENT ANIMAL _____

FAMILY MEMBER #1 _____

FAMILY MEMBER #2 _____

VERB THAT ENDS IN -ING _____

A DIFFERENT FOOD _____

The Perfect Picnic Spot

Use the words from the previous page to complete a silly story.

When my family suggested having our lunch at the Rattlesnake Springs, I was

_____. I love eating my _____ outside! I knew we had picked up a
EMOTION   FOOD

box of _____ from the _____ for after lunch, my favorite. We drove up
SOMETHING SWEET   STORE

to the area and I jumped out of the _____. "I will find the perfect spot for
                              MODE OF TRANSPORTATION

a picnic!" I grabbed a _____ for us to sit on, and I ran off. I passed a picnic
                    NOUN

table, but it was covered with _____ so we couldn't sit there. The next
                        SOMETHING ALIVE

picnic table looked okay, but there were smears of _____ and pieces of
                                         SAUCE

_____ everywhere. The people that were there before must have been
PLURAL VEGETABLES

_____! I gritted my _____ together and kept walking down the path,
ADJECTIVE   PLURAL BODY PART

determined to find the perfect spot. I wanted a table with a good view of the

springs. Why was this so hard? If we were lucky, I might even get to see _____
                                                          ANIMAL

eating some _____ on the cliffside. They don't have those in _____, where
         PLURAL FRUIT   PLACE

I am from. I walked down a little hill and there it was, the perfect spot! The

trees towered overhead and looked as tall as _____. The patch of grass
                                    SOMETHING TALL

was a beautiful _____ color. The _____ flowers were growing on
            COLOR   ADJECTIVE

the side of a _____. I looked across the deserts plain and even saw a
          NOUN

_____ on the edge of a rock. I looked back to see my _____ and
DIFFERENT ANIMAL   FAMILY MEMBER #1

_____ _____ a picnic basket. "I hope you brought plenty of
FAMILY MEMBER #2 VERB THAT ENDS IN ING

_____, I'm starving!"
A DIFFERENT FOOD   29

Hike to a Cavern

start
here

DID YOU KNOW?
Secretly tucked below the desert terrain are more than 119 known caves formed when sulfuric acid dissolved the surrounding limestone.

Bat Flight Program
Word Search

From late May to October, visitors to Carlsbad Caverns can participate in the Ranger led talk about bats before their flight. From the Bat Flight Amphitheater, visitors can witness thousands of Brazilian free-tailed bats emerge from Carlsbad Cavern in search of food.

1. cavern
2. amphitheater
3. summer
4. darkness
5. night
6. wingspan
7. insect
8. evening
9. emerge
10. dives
11. migration
12. out flight
13. Brazilian
14. free-tailed
15. mammals
16. roost
17. colony

```
D I V E S U L S S E N K R A D
O A D A U I A Z S W I R W R H
U V D N M I T T A W G L K O A
T E U D M P S U C Y H T B M L
F I N S E C T A L E T R S K C
L P D L R E T A E H T I P M A
I O S E M R C E V H L R L I V
G R B E M K I R E I L S V G E
H T R O O S T O N O U D E R R
T G I R S M O W I N G S P A N
E S M U A T I C N L K B N T N
S H N A K A O I G A S K T I E
T J O S M H I N Z Y N O L O C
E Y G E L M V E I N D R V N O
R W E L D N A I L L I Z A R B
T T E L G R E L N L A K E N T
U A E E S A E N S O A P V E B
C J D E L I A T E E R F I O N
```

31

Leave No Trace Quiz

Leave No Trace is a concept that helps people make decisions during outdoor recreation that protects the environment. There are seven principles that guide us when we spend time outdoors, whether you are in a national park or not. Are you an expert in Leave No Trace? Take this quiz and find out!

1. How can you plan ahead and prepare to ensure you have the best experience you can in the national park?
   a. Make sure you stop by the ranger station for a map and to ask about current conditions.
   b. Just wing it! You will know the best trail when you see it.
   c. Stick to your plan, even if conditions change. You traveled a long way to get here, and you should stick to your plan.
2. What is an example of traveling on a durable surface?
   a. Walking only on the designated path.
   b. Walking on the grass that borders the trail if the trail is very muddy.
   c. Taking a shortcut if you can find one because it means you will be walking less.
3. Why should you dispose of waste properly?
   a. You don't need to. Park rangers love to pick up the trash you leave behind.
   b. You should actually leave your leftovers behind, because animals will eat them. It is important to make sure they aren't hungry.
   c. So that other peoples' experiences of the park are not impacted by you leaving your waste behind.
4. How can you best follow the concept "leave what you find?"
   a. Take only a small rock or leaf to remember your trip.
   b. Take pictures, but leave any physical items where they are.
   c. Leave everything you find, unless it may be rare like an arrowhead, then it is okay to take.
5. What is not a good example of minimizing campfire impacts?
   a. Only having a campfire in a pre-existing campfire ring.
   b. Checking in with current conditions when you consider making a campfire.
   c. Building a new campfire ring in a location that has a better view.
6. What is a poor example of respecting wildlife?
   a. Building squirrel houses out of rocks so the squirrels have a place to live.
   b. Stay far away from wildlife and give them plenty of space.
   c. Reminding your grown-ups not to drive too fast in animal habitats while visiting the park.
7. How can you show consideration of other visitors?
   a. Play music on your speaker so other people at the campground can enjoy it.
   b. Wear headphones on the trail if you choose to listen to music.
   c. Make sure to yell "Hello!" to every animal you see at top volume.

Take a Hike

Go for a hike with your friends or family. If you aren't able to visit Carlsbad Caverns National Park, go for a walk in a park near where you live. Read through the prompts before your walk and finish the activities after you return.

Draw something you saw that moves:

Draw something you saw when you looked up:

Draw something you saw that grows out of the ground:

Draw a picture of your favorite part of the walk:

Weather Watch

Find a place in an open area above ground where you can easily see the sky. Complete the activities below to provide your weather report. If you aren't in the park, you can do this activity from home.

Can you feel any wind?

What does the sky look like?

Is there anything you notice about the weather today?

What is the date?

What is the time?

Where is the sun in the sky? (rising, midpoint, falling)

What direction is the wind blowing?

Are there clouds in the sky? If so, draw them below:

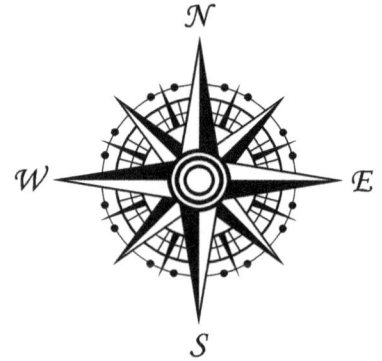

Navigate the Calcite Column

start here →

Columns are just one type of formation you might encounter at Carlsbad Caverns. They occur when stalactites and stalagmites fuse together.

Formations like columns, soda straws, and draperies are called speleothems. Their growth is slow, occurring over thousands and millions of years.

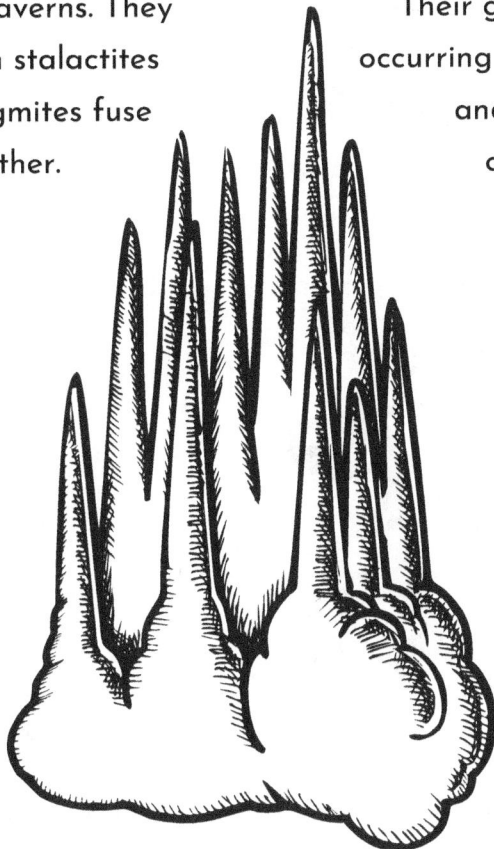

Stacking Rocks

Have you ever seen stacks of rocks while hiking in national parks? Do you know what they are or what they mean? These rock piles are called cairns and often mark hiking routes in parks. Every park has a different way to maintain trails and cairns. However, they all have the same rule: If you come across a cairn, do not disturb it!

Color the cairn and the rules to remember.

1. Do not tamper with cairns.

If a cairn is tampered with or an unauthorized one is built, then future visitors may become disoriented or even lost.

2. Do not build unauthorized cairns.

Moving rocks disturbs the soil and makes the area more prone to erosion. Disturbing rocks can disturb fragile plants.

3. Do not add to existing cairns.

Authorized cairns are carefully designed. Adding to them can actually cause them to collapse.

Decoding Using American Sign Language

American Sign Language, also called ASL for short, is a language that many Deaf people or people who are hard of hearing use to communicate. People use ASL to communicate with their hands. Did you know people from all over the country and world travel to national parks? You may hear people speaking other languages. You might also see people using ASL. Use the American Manual Alphabet chart to decode some national parks facts.

This was the first national park to be established:

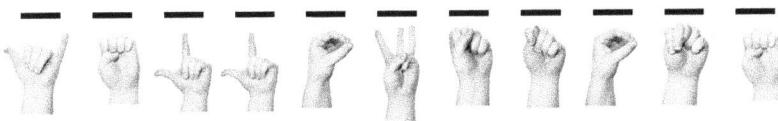

_ _ _ _ _ _ _ _ _ _

This is the biggest national park in the US:

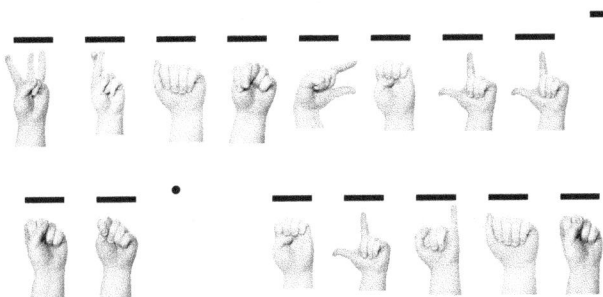

_ _ _ _ _ _ _ _ _ -

_ _ _ . _ _ _ _

This is the most visited national park:

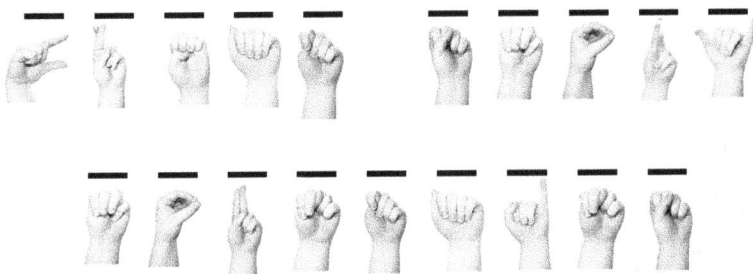

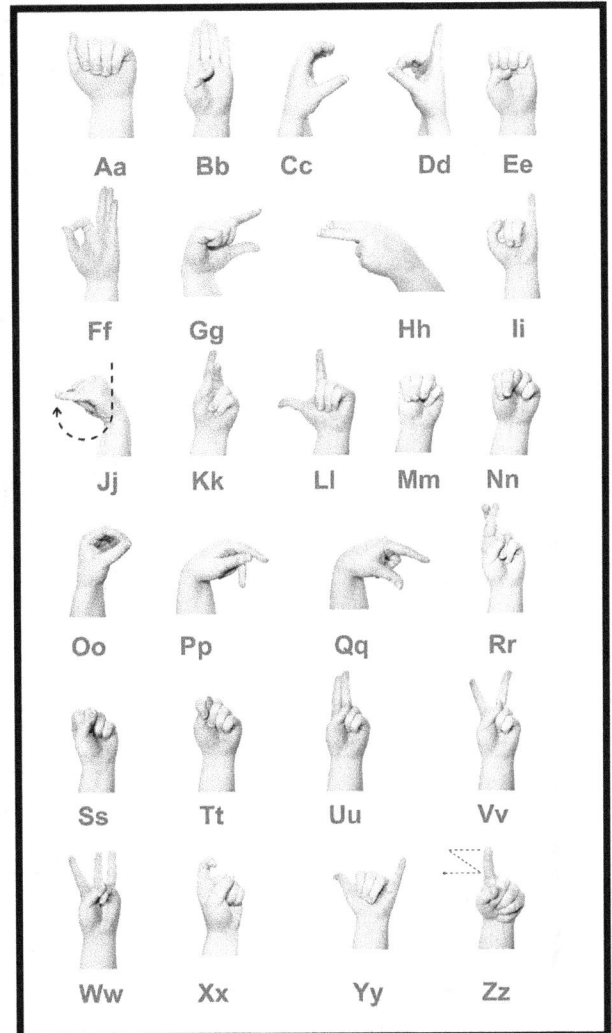

_ _ _ _ _ _ _ _ _

_ _ _ _ _ _ _

Aa	Bb	Cc	Dd	Ee
Ff	Gg		Hh	Ii
Jj	Kk	Ll	Mm	Nn
Oo	Pp		Qq	Rr
Ss	Tt		Uu	Vv
Ww	Xx		Yy	Zz

Hint: Pay close attention to the position of the thumb!

Try it! Using the chart, try to make the letters of the alphabet with your hand. What is the hardest letter to make? Can you spell out your name? Show a friend or family member and have them watch you spell out the name of the national park you are in.

Go Birdwatching at Juniper Ridge Trail

start here

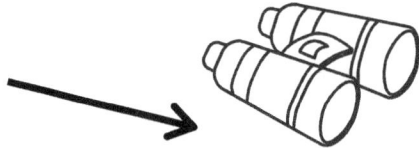

Butterflies of the Carlsbad Caverns

Dozens of species of butterflies and moths live in Carlsbad Caverns National Park. Their wingspan size varies, as do the patterns on their wings. Design your own butterfly below. Make sure the wings are symmetrical, which means both sides match.

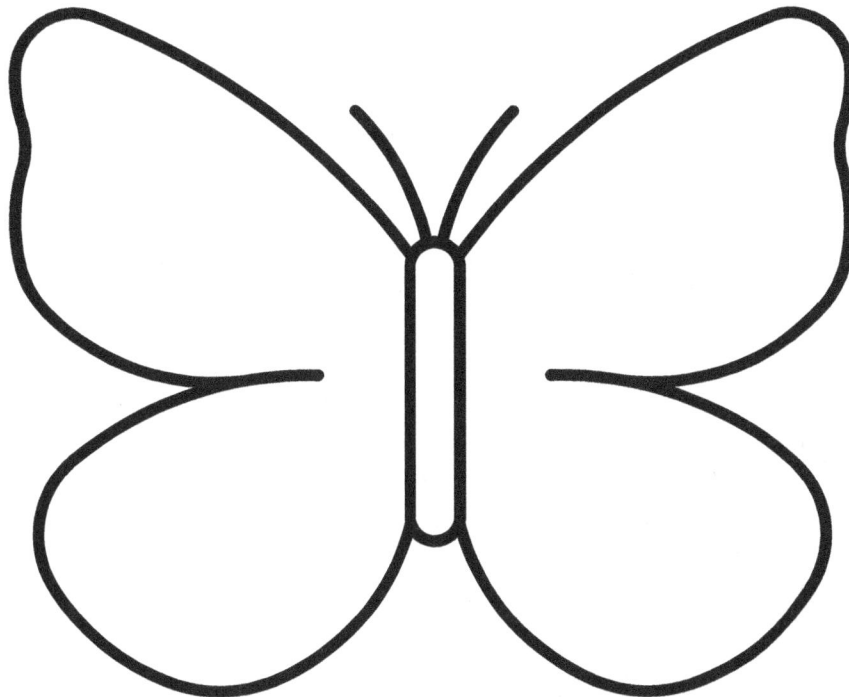

A Hike at Walnut Canyon

Fill in the blanks on this page without looking at the full story. Once you have each line filled out, use the words you've chosen to complete the story on the next page.

ADJECTIVE _

SOMETHING TO EAT _

SOMETHING TO DRINK _

NOUN _

ARTICLE OF CLOTHING _

BODY PART _

VERB _

ANIMAL _

SAME TYPE OF FOOD _

ADJECTIVE _

SAME ANIMAL _

VERB THAT ENDS IN "ED" _

NUMBER _

A DIFFERENT NUMBER _

SOMETHING THAT FLIES _

LIGHT SOURCE _

PLURAL NOUN _

FAMILY MEMBER _

YOUR NICKNAME _

A Hike at Walnut Canyon

Use the words from the previous page to complete a silly story.

I went for a hike at Walnut Canyon today. In my favorite _____
ADJECTIVE

backpack, I made sure to pack a map so I wouldn't get lost. I also threw in an

extra _____ just in case I got hungry and a bottle of _____.
SOMETHING TO EAT   SOMETHING TO DRINK

I put on my _____ spray, and I tied a _____ around my
NOUN   ARTICLE OF CLOTHING

_____, in case it gets chilly. I started to _____ down the path. As
BODY PART   VERB

soon as I turned the corner, I came face to face with a(n) _____. I think
ANIMAL

it was as startled as I was! What should I do? I had to think fast! Should I

give it some of my _____? No. I had to remember what the
SAME TYPE OF FOOD

_____ ranger told me: "If you see one, back away slowly and try not to
ADJECTIVE

scare it." Soon enough, the _____ _____ away. The coast
SAME ANIMAL   VERB THAT ENDS IN ED

was clear. _____ hours later, I finally got to the lookout. I felt like I could
NUMBER

see for a _____ miles. I took a picture of a _____ so I could always
A DIFFERENT NUMBER   NOUN

remember this moment. As I was putting my camera away, a _____
SOMETHING THAT FLIES

flew by, reminding me that it was almost nighttime. I turned on my

_____ and headed back. I could hear the _____ singing their
LIGHT SOURCE   PLURAL INSECT

evening song. Just as I was getting tired, I saw my _____ and our tent.
FAMILY MEMBER

"Welcome back _____! How was your hike?"
NICKNAME

Rock Scavenger Hunt

Pay close attention to the things beneath your feet. If you visit Carlsbad Caverns National Park, you will see all sorts of rocks, both big and small. Go on a rock hunt! You may have to get close to the ground and focus carefully to be able to find all the rocks on this list.

☐ A sharp rock   ☐ A smooth rock

☐ A flat rock   ☐ A small rock

☐ A round rock   ☐ A huge rock

☐ A rectangular rock   ☐ A rough rock

☐ A dull rock   ☐ A shiny rock

☐ A rock with stripes   ☐ A rock with speckles

☐ A multicolored rock   ☐ A rock with only one color

Compare two rocks that look very different from each other.
What makes them different? Think about their size, their shape, their texture, and their color.
Do they have any similarities?

_____

_____

_____

Let's Go Camping
Word Search

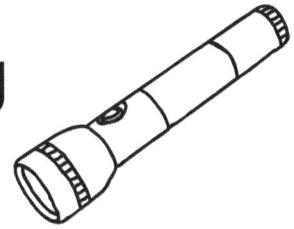

Words may be horizontal, vertical, diagonal, or they might even be backwards!

1. tent
2. camp stove
3. sleeping bag
4. bug spray
5. sunscreen
6. map
7. flashlight
8. pillow
9. lantern
10. ice
11. snacks
12. smores
13. water
14. first aid kit
15. chair
16. cards
17. books
18. games
19. trail
20. hat

```
D P P I L L O W D B T E A C I
E O A D P R E A A M B R C A N
P W C A M P S T O V E I H X G
R A H S G E L E B E E D A P S
E L B U G S P R A Y N G I E A
S I A H G C I C N N M E R C N
C W N L A F I R S K O O B F K
M T A E M I L E L H M R W L J
T A P R E A O R E S L B A A B
S M P A S R R T E N T L U S C
C E A I I R C G P E I U J H A
S S N A C K S S I M O K I L R
I J R S F O I S N J R A Q I D
C Y E T L E V E G U O R V G S
E W T A K C A B B S S O H H M
X J N F I R S T A I D K I T T
U A A E S S E N G E T P V A B
C J L I A R T D N A M A H A S
```

43

All in the Day of a Park Ranger

Park Rangers are hardworking individuals dedicated to protecting our parks, monuments, museums, and more. They take care of the natural and cultural resources for future generations. Rangers also help protect the visitors of the park. Their responsibilities are broad and they work both with the public and behind the scenes.

What have you seen park rangers do? Use your knowledge of the duties of park rangers to fill out a typical daily schedule, listing one activity for each hour. Feel free to make up your own, but some examples of activities are provided on the right. Read carefully! Not all the example activities are befitting a ranger.

6 am	Lead a sunrise hike
7 am	
8 am	
9 am	
10 am	
11 am	
12 pm	Enjoy a lunch break outside
1 pm	
2 pm	
3 pm	
4 pm	Teach visitors about the geology of the caves
5 pm	
6 pm	
7 pm	
8 pm	
9 pm	

- feed the migratory birds
- build trails for visitors to enjoy
- throw rocks off the side of the mountain
- rescue lost hikers
- study animal behavior
- record air quality data
- answer questions at the visitor center
- pick wildflowers
- pick up litter
- share marshmallows with squirrels
- repair handrails
- lead a class on a field trip
- catch frogs or toads and make them race
- lead people on educational hikes
- write articles for the park website
- protect the river from pollution
- remove non-native plants from the park
- study how climate change is affecting the park
- give a talk about mountain lions
- lead a program for campers on bats

If you were a park ranger, which of the above tasks would you enjoy most?

_____

_____

Draw Yourself as a Park Ranger

RANGER

Bats of Carlsbad Caverns

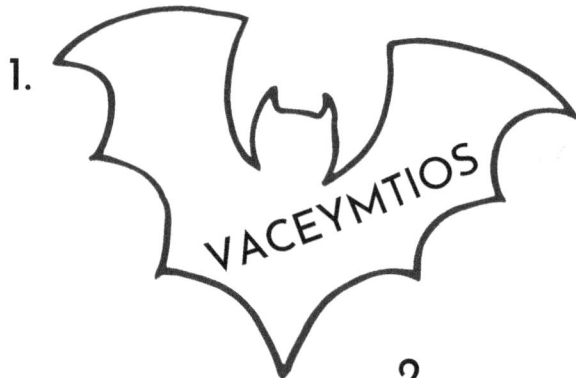

1. VACEYMTIOS

2. RDE TEEASRN

3. BWORBGIN

4. RYOAH

5. APLILD

Unscramble the names of these bats that live in the park.

1. _____
2. _____
3. _____
4. _____
5. _____

Word Bank

hoary
big brown
fringed myotis
pallid
eastern red
cave myotis
silver-haired
yuma myotis

46

Amphibians

One species of toad and five species of frogs live in Carlsbad Caverns Park. Even more types of salamanders live there too. Frogs and toads both spend the beginning of their lives the same way - as tadpoles. Tadpoles hatch from eggs, usually in springs or pools of water.

Both frogs and toads are amphibians. Salamanders are amphibians too. Color the amphibians below.

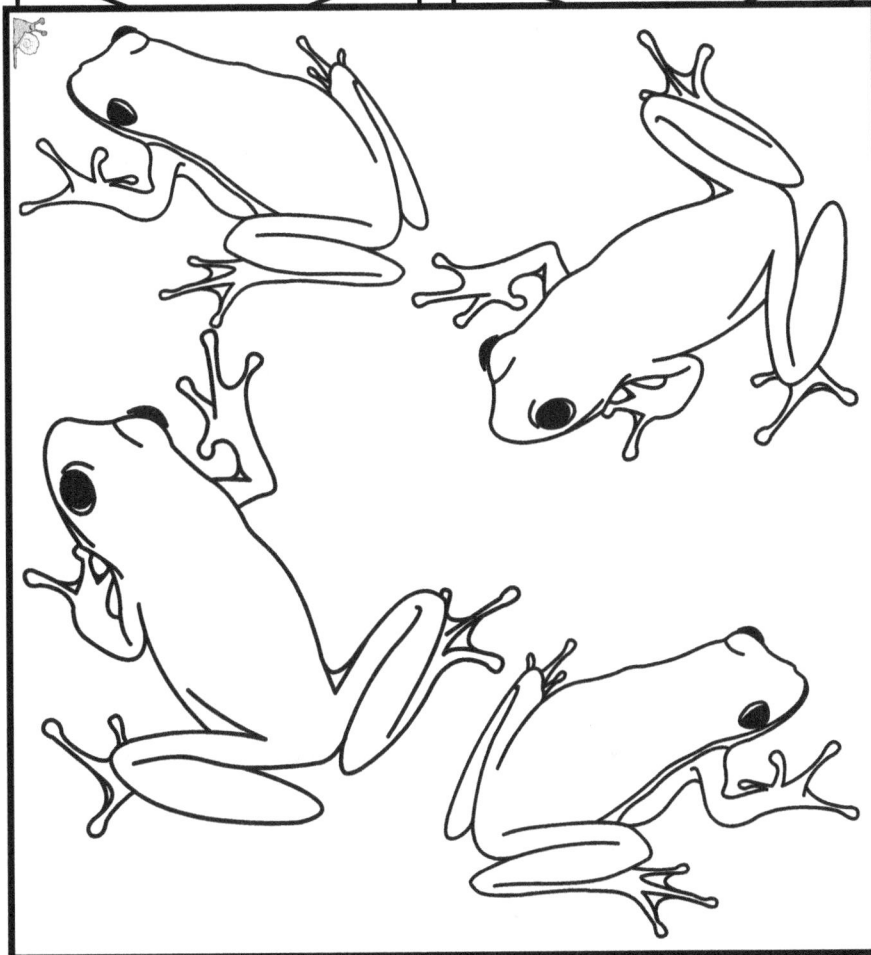

Sound Exploration

Spend a minute or two listening to all of the sounds around you.
Draw your favorite sound.

How did this sound make you feel?

_____

_____

What did you think when you heard this sound?

_____

_____

Take in the Teeny-Tiny

Take a walk through the desert and draw examples of teensy things you can find such as little plants, bugs, and pebbles.

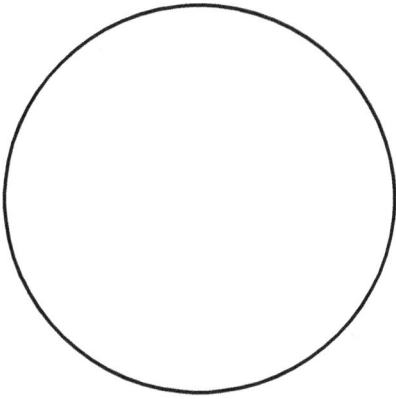

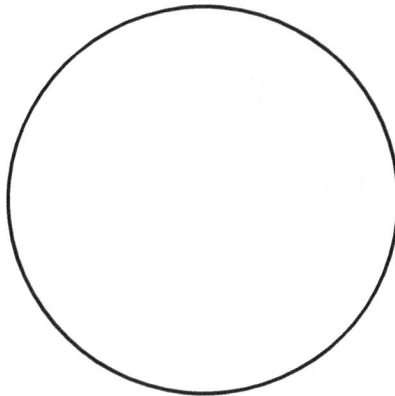

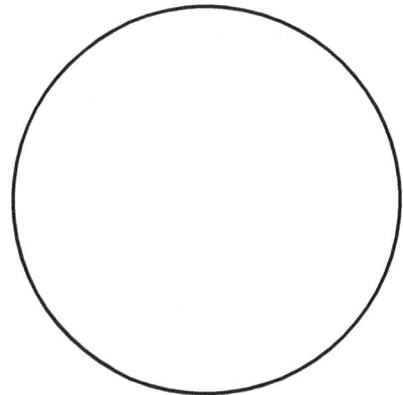

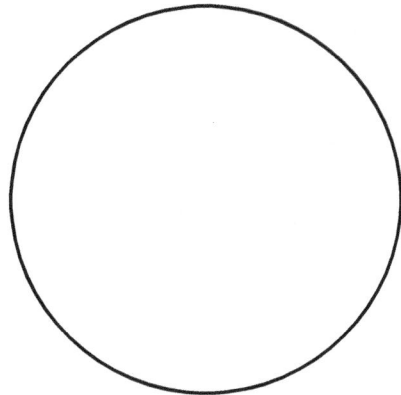

63 National Parks

How many other national parks have you been to? Which one do you want to visit next? Note that if some of these parks fall on the border of more than one state, you may check it off more than once!

Alaska
- ☐ Denali National Park
- ☐ Gates of the Arctic National Park
- ☐ Glacier Bay National Park
- ☐ Katmai National Park
- ☐ Kenai Fjords National Park
- ☐ Kobuk Valley National Park
- ☐ Lake Clark National Park
- ☐ Wrangell-St. Elias National Park

American Samoa
- ☐ National Park of American Samoa

Arizona
- ☐ Grand Canyon National Park
- ☐ Petrified Forest National Park
- ☐ Saguaro National Park

Arkansas
- ☐ Hot Springs National Park

California
- ☐ Channel Islands National Park
- ☐ Death Valley National Park
- ☐ Joshua Tree National Park
- ☐ Kings Canyon National Park
- ☐ Lassen Volcanic National Park
- ☐ Pinnacles National Park
- ☐ Redwood National Park
- ☐ Sequoia National Park
- ☐ Yosemite National Park

Colorado
- ☐ Black Canyon of the Gunnison National Park
- ☐ Great Sand Dunes National Park
- ☐ Mesa Verde National Park
- ☐ Rocky Mountain National Park

Florida
- ☐ Biscayne National Park
- ☐ Dry Tortugas National Park
- ☐ Everglades National Park

Hawaii
- ☐ Haleakalā National Park
- ☐ Hawai'i Volcanoes National Park

Idaho
- ☐ Yellowstone National Park

Kentucky
- ☐ Mammoth Cave National Park

Indiana
- ☐ Indiana Dunes National Park

Maine
- ☐ Acadia National Park

Michigan
- ☐ Isle Royale National Park

Minnesota
- ☐ Voyageurs National Park

Missouri
- ☐ Gateway Arch National Park

Montana
- ☐ Glacier National Park
- ☐ Yellowstone National Park

Nevada
- ☐ Death Valley National Park
- ☐ Great Basin National Park

New Mexico
- ☐ Carlsbad Caverns National Park
- ☐ White Sands National Park

North Dakota
- ☐ Theodore Roosevelt National Park

North Carolina
- ☐ Great Smoky Mountains National Park

Ohio
- ☐ Cuyahoga Valley National Park

Oregon
- ☐ Crater Lake National Park

South Carolina
- ☐ Congaree National Park

South Dakota
- ☐ Badlands National Park
- ☐ Wind Cave National Park

Tennessee
- ☐ Great Smoky Mountains National Park

Texas
- ☐ Big Bend National Park
- ☐ Guadalupe Mountains National Park

Utah
- ☐ Arches National Park
- ☐ Bryce Canyon National Park
- ☐ Canyonlands National Park
- ☐ Capitol Reef National Park
- ☐ Zion National Park

Virgin Islands
- ☐ Virgin Islands National Park

Virginia
- ☐ Shenandoah National Park

Washington
- ☐ Mount Rainier National Park
- ☐ North Cascades National Park
- ☐ Olympic National Park

West Virginia
- ☐ New River Gorge National Park

Wyoming
- ☐ Grand Teton National Park
- ☐ Yellowstone National Park

Other National Parks Crossword

Besides Carlsbad Caverns National Park, there are 62 other diverse and beautiful national parks across the United States. Try your hand at this crossword. If you need help, look at the previous page for some hints.

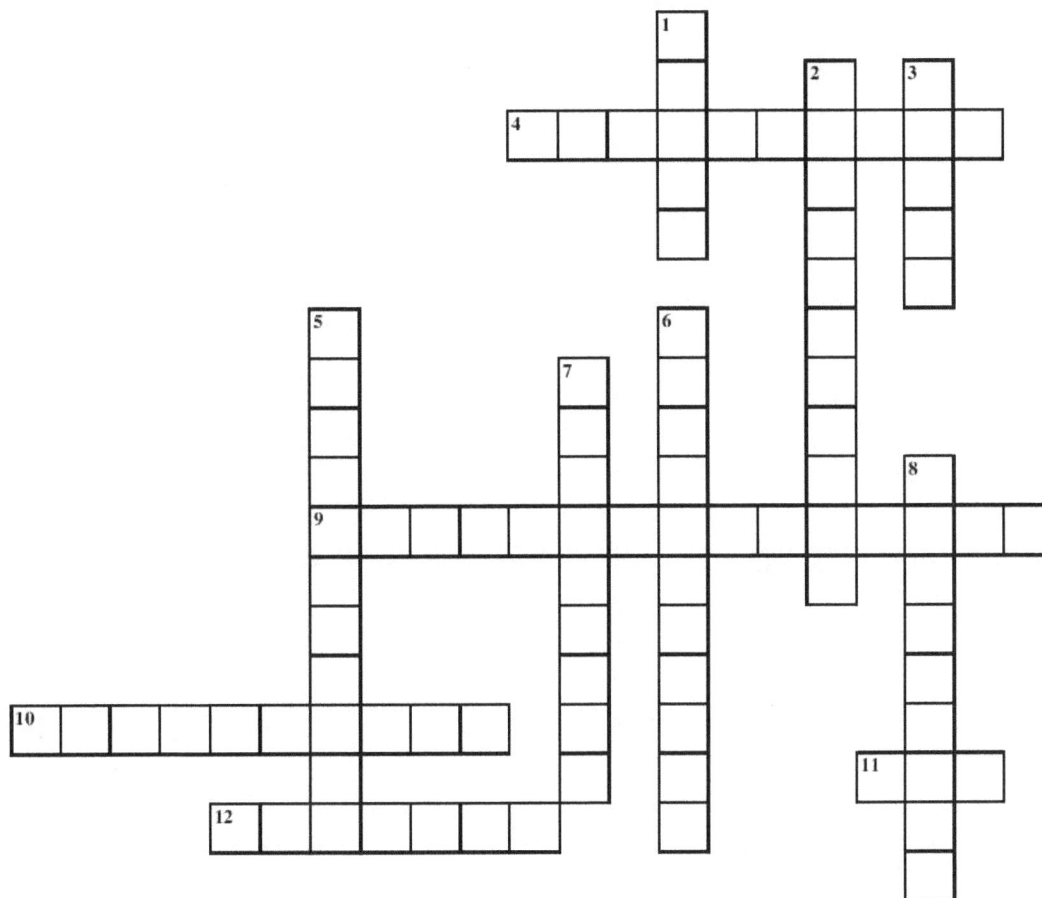

Down

1. State where Acadia National Park is located
2. This national park has the Spanish word for turtle in it
3. Number of national parks in Alaska
5. This national park has some of the hottest temperatures in the world
6. This national park is the only one in Idaho
7. This toothsome creature can famously be found in Everglades National Park
8. Only president with a national park named for them

Across

4. This state has the most national parks
9. This park has some of the newest land in the US, caused by volcanic eruptions
10. This park has the deepest lake in the United States
11. This color shows up in the name of a national park in California
12. This national park deserves a gold medal

Which National Park Will You Go To Next?
Word Search

1. Zion
2. Big Bend
3. Glacier
4. Olympic
5. Sequoia
6. Bryce
7. Mesa Verde
8. Biscayne
9. Wind Cave
10. Great Basin
11. Katmai
12. Yellowstone
13. Voyageurs
14. Arches
15. Badlands
16. Denali
17. Glacier Bay
18. Hot Springs

```
F M M E S A V E R D E B N E Y
E A B I G B E N D E S A S E M
Y L I C A L O Y N E E D L T G
D M G A S S A U C N R L U E R
C E L I I T S C R E O A A K E
S N A W Y E E O I W T N A C A
G I C H A A Q C S E M D N S T
N O I Z P R U T I M R S N E B
I W E L M P O N B W E B K H A
R J R F D N I F L I H B U C S
P A B E E S A N E S O P W R I
S J A E N Y A C S I B A U A N
T C Y I A D O H H Y M E A L R
O T A T L M L E S E G R W R J
H S T O I K A T M A I R O P B
I C H U R C O L Y M P I C O U
O Y G T S D E O S B R Y C E T
W I N D C A V E I N R O H E M
```

Field Notes

Spend some time reflecting on your trip to Carlsbad Caverns National Park. Your field notes will help you remember the things you experienced. Use the space below to write about your day.

While I was at Carlsbad Caverns National Park...

I saw:

_____

_____

_____

_____

I heard:

_____

_____

_____

I felt:

_____

_____

Draw a picture of your favorite thing in the park.

I wondered:

_____

_____

_____

_____

ANSWER KEY

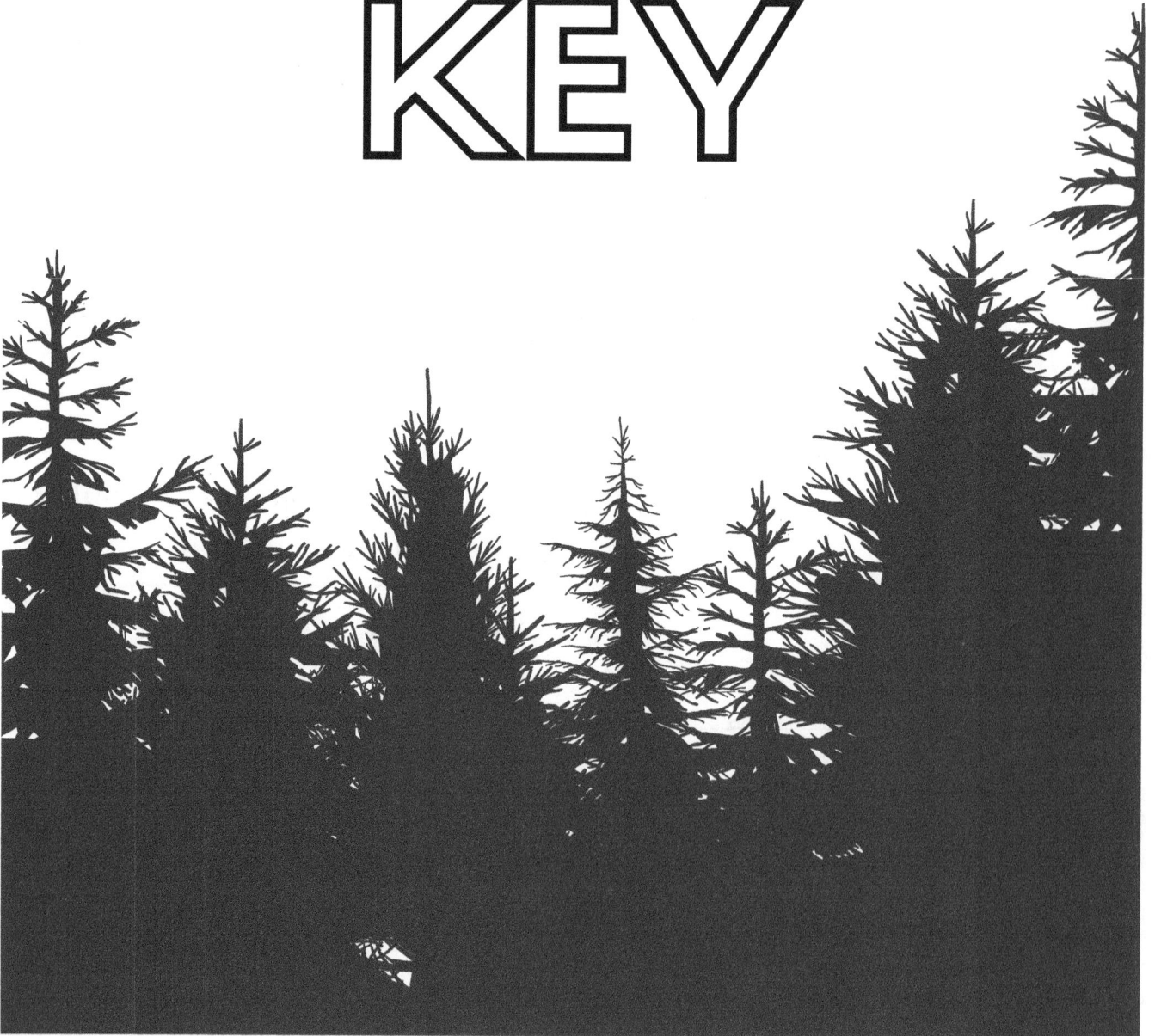

Go Horseback Riding on the Guadalupe Ridge Trail

Help find the horse's lost shoe!

start here →

DID YOU KNOW?

Horseback riding is a popular activity in Carlsbad Caverns National Park. There are many trails that you can take horses for day or overnight trips.

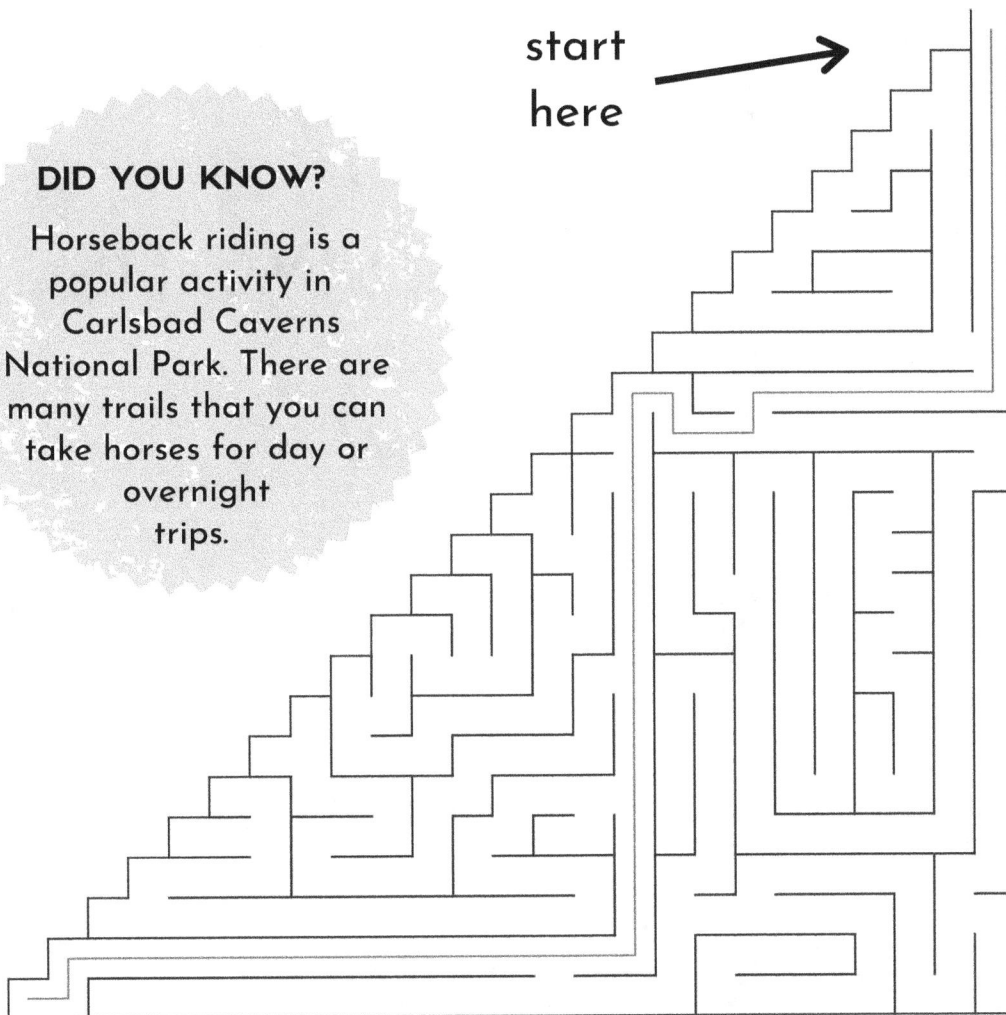

Answers: Who lives here?

Below are 8 plants and animals that live in the park.
Use the word bank to fill in the clues below.

WORD BANK: BADGER, BUFFALOBUR, WILLET, YUMA MYOTIS,
RACCOON, SPARROW, PIPISTRELLE, TEXAS TOAD

RAC C OON

YUM A ■ MYOTIS

SPAR R OW

WIL L ET

PIPI S TRELLE

BUFFALO B UR

TEX A S ■ TOAD

BA D GER

Find the Match!
Common Names and Latin Names

Match the common name to the scientific name for each animal. The first one is done for you. Use clues on the page before and after this one to complete the matches.

Elk   Aquila chrysaetos

Wester Water Hemlock   Ursus americanus

Torrey Yucca   Actitis macularius

American Black Bear   Lampropeltis getula

Great Horned Owl   Cicuta douglasii

Golden Eagle   Myotis velifer

Spotted Sandpiper   Bubo virginianus

Desert Kingsnake   Cervus canadensis

Cave Myotis   Yucca torreyi

Golden Eagle

Aquila chrysaetos

Jumbles Answers

1. S TARGAZING

2. HIKING

3. BIRDING

4. CAMPING

5. PICNICKING

6. SIGHTSEEING

7. CAVE EXPLORING

Helping Bats Thrive Code Answer

clean your shoes, clothes, and gear before and after going into any cave.

National Park Emblem Answers

1. This represents all plants: **Sequoia Tree**

2. This represents all animals: **Bison**

3. This represents the landscapes: **Mountains**

4. This represents the waters protected by the park service: **Water**

5. This represents the historical and archeological values: **Arrowhead**

Answers: The Ten Essentials

Careful preparation and knowledge are key to a successful adventure into Carlsbad Caverns backcountry.

The ten essentials are a list of things that are important to have when you go for longer hikes. If you go on a hike to the <u>backcountry</u>, it is especially important that you have everything you need in case of an emergency. If you get lost or something unforeseen happens, it is good to be prepared to survive until help finds you.

The ten essentials list was developed in the 1930s by an outdoors group called the Mountaineers. Over time and technological advancements, this list has evolved. Can you identify all the things on the current list? Circle each of the "essentials" and cross out everything that doesn't make the cut.

(circled) fire: matches, lighter, tinder, and/or stove	(crossed out) a pint of milk	(crossed out) extra money	(circled) headlamp, plus extra batteries	(circled) extra clothes
(circled) extra water	(crossed out) a dog	(crossed out) Polaroid camera	(crossed out) bug net	(crossed out) lightweight games, such as a deck of cards
(circled) extra food	(crossed out) a roll of duct tape	(circled) shelter	(circled) sun protection such as sunglasses, sun-protective clothes and sunscreen	(circled) knife, plus a gear repair kit
(crossed out) a mirror	(circled) navigation: map, compass, altimeter, GPS device, or satellite messenger	(circled) first aid kit	(crossed out) extra flip-flops	(crossed out) entertainment such as video games or books

Backcountry - a remote undeveloped rural area.

Carlsbad Caverns Word Search

Words may be horizontal, vertical, diagonal,
or they might even be backwards!

1. caves
2. bat
3. elevator
4. New Mexico
5. balloon ballroom
6. guano
7. cave swallow
8. bat cave
9. deer
10. stalagmite
11. flowstone
12. lily pads
13. popcorn
14. draperies
15. Pinchot
16. Lechuguilla
17. sotol
18. Jim White
19. mining
20. Guadalupe

```
B A L L O O N B A L L R O O M
H A A S K I L O C E E L D N J
T E T R A A O S C C A V E S B
S M I N I N G S C H R L E C C
T E A D I A B L O U I U R A L
A O L D T O N A U G T E A S I
L E E P U L A D A U G R I C N
A L B A M O I E P I N C H O T
G E P R O T A V E L E D Y D E
M C O C C O O Y H L W G J E N
I T P H C S I N O A M E I S O
T R C I K O E I S B E K M R T
E I O S H Z I R A I X A W G S
J C R O L O V T S O C R H E W
N I N A K M C N E R O L I E O
L I L Y P A D S L Z E S T N L
H Y D R V D R A P E R I E S F
C A V E S W A L L O W A L A M
```

60

Wildlife Wisdom

The national park is home to many different kinds of animals. Seeing wildlife can be an exciting part of visiting the national park but it is important to remember that these animals are wild. They need plenty of space and a healthy habitat where they can find their own food. Part of this is not allowing animals to eat any human food. This is their home and we are the visitors. We need to be respectful of the wildlife in the park.

Directions: Circle the highlighted words that best complete the following sentences.

If an animal changes its behavior because of your presence, you are:
 A) too close
 B) funny looking
 C) dehydrated and should drink more water

The best thing we can do to help wild animals survive is:
 A) make them pets
 B) protect their habitat
 C) knit them winter sweaters

In a national park, it is okay to share your food with wild animals:
 A) never
 B) always
 C) sometimes

When you're hiking in an area where there are bears, you should warn bears that you are entering their space by:
 A) hiking quietly
 B) making noise
 C) wearing bright colors

At night, park rangers care for the animals by:
 A) putting them back into their cages
 B) tucking them into bed
 C) leaving them alone

If you see an abandoned bird's nest, it is best to:
 A) pet the baby birds
 B) leave it alone
 C) crunch the empty eggshells

Bears look under logs in hopes of finding:
 A) granola bars
 B) insects
 C) peanuts to eat

The place where an animal lives is called its:
 A) condo
 B) habitat
 C) crib

61

Solution: Hike to a Cavern

DID YOU KNOW? Secretly tucked below the desert terrain are more than 119 known caves formed when sulfuric acid dissolved the surrounding limestone.

Bat Flight Program
Word Search

From late May to October, visitors to Carlsbad Caverns can participate in the Ranger led talk about bats before their flight. From the Bat Flight Amphitheater, visitors can witness thousands of Brazilian free-tailed bats emerge from Carlsbad Cavern in search of food.

1. cavern
2. amphitheater
3. summer
4. darkness
5. night
6. wingspan
7. insect
8. evening
9. emerge
10. dives
11. migration
12. out flight
13. Brazilian
14. free-tailed
15. mammals
16. roost
17. colony

```
D I V E S U L S S E N K R A D
O A D A U I A Z S W I R W R H
U V D N M I T T A W G L K O A
T E U D M P S U C Y H T B M L
F I N S E C T A L E T R S K C
L P D L R E T A E H T I P M A
I O S E M R C E V H L R L I V
G R B E M K I R E I L S V G E
H T R O O S T O N O U D E R R
T G I R S M O W I N G S P A N
E S M U A T I C N L K B N T N
S H N A K A O I G A S K T I E
T J O S M H I N Z Y N O L O C
E Y G E L M V E I N D R V N O
R W E L D N A I L L I Z A R B
T T E L G R E L N L A K E N T
U A E E S A E N S O A P V E B
C J D E L I A T E E R F I O N
```

63

Answers: Leave No Trace Quiz

Leave No Trace is a concept that helps people make decisions during outdoor recreation that protects the environment. There are seven principles that guide us when we spend time outdoors, whether you are in a national park or not. Are you an expert in Leave No Trace? Take this quiz and find out!

1. How can you plan ahead and prepare to ensure you have the best experience you can in the National Park?
   A. Make sure you stop by the ranger station for a map and to ask about current conditions.
2. What is an example of traveling on a durable surface?
   A. Walking only on the designated path.
3. Why should you dispose of waste properly?
   C. So that other peoples' experiences of the park are not impacted by you leaving your waste behind.
4. How can you best follow the concept "leave what you find?"
   B. Take pictures but leave any physical items where they are.
5. What is not a good example of minimizing campfire impacts?
   C. Building a new campfire ring in a location that has a better view.
6. What is a poor example of respecting wildlife?
   A. Building squirrel houses out of rocks from the river so the squirrels have a place to live.
7. How can you show consideration of other visitors?
   B. Wear headphones on the trail if you choose to listen to music.

Navigate the Calcite Column

start here →

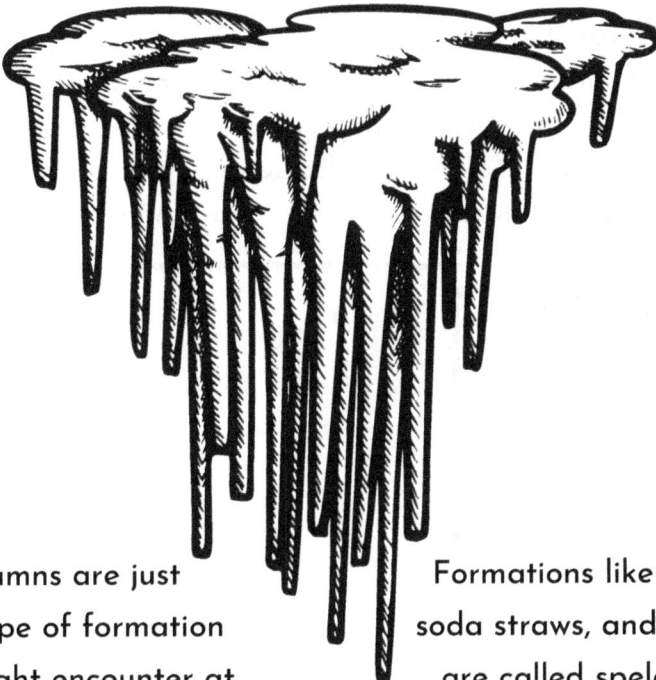

Columns are just one type of formation you might encounter at Carlsbad Caverns. They occur when stalactites and stalagmites fuse together.

Formations like columns, soda straws, and draperies are called speleothems. Their growth is slow, occurring over thousands and millions of years.

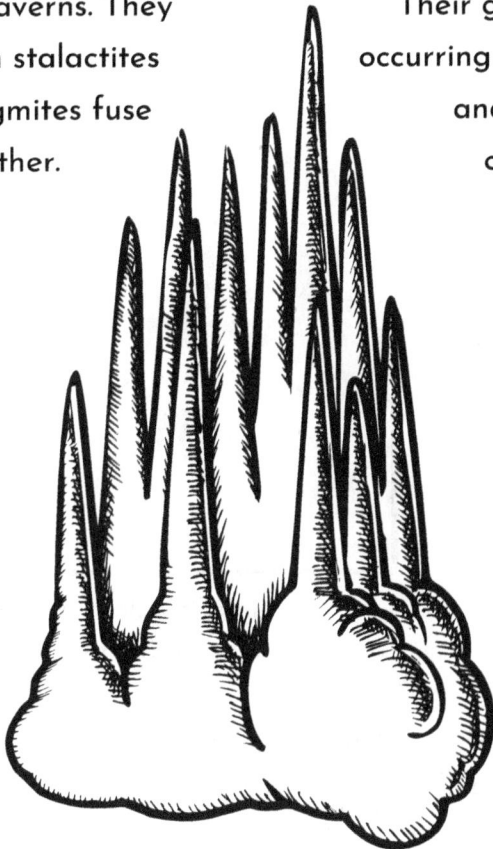

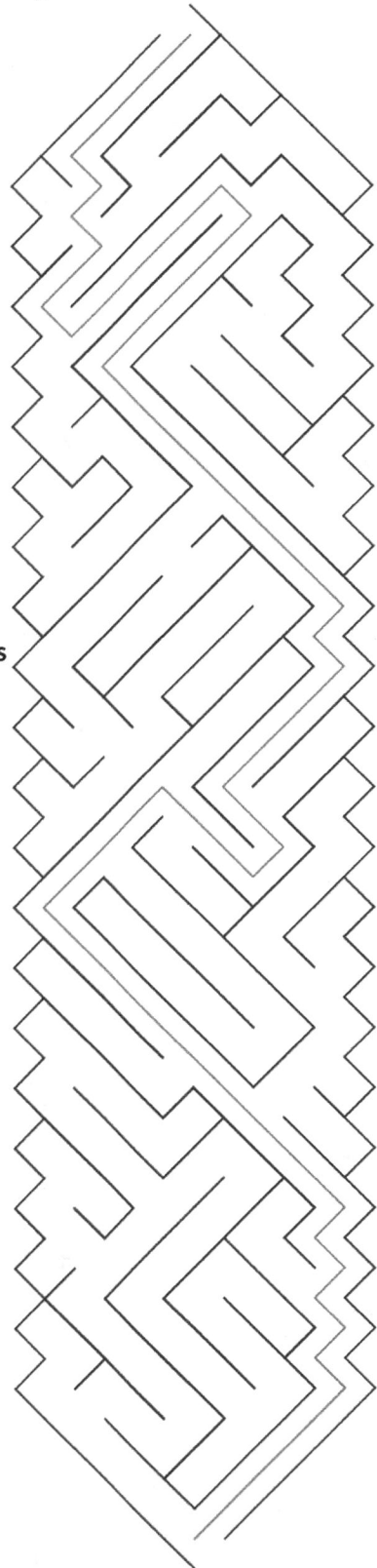

Decoding Using American Sign Language

American Sign Language, also called ASL for short, is a language that many Deaf people or people who are hard of hearing use to communicate. People use ASL to communicate with their hands. Did you know people from all over the country and world travel to national parks? You may hear people speaking other languages. You might also see people using ASL. Use the American Manual Alphabet chart to decode some national parks facts.

This was the first national park to be established:

Y E L L O W S T O N E

This is the biggest national park in the US:

W R A N G E L L -

S T . E L I A S

This is the most visited national park:

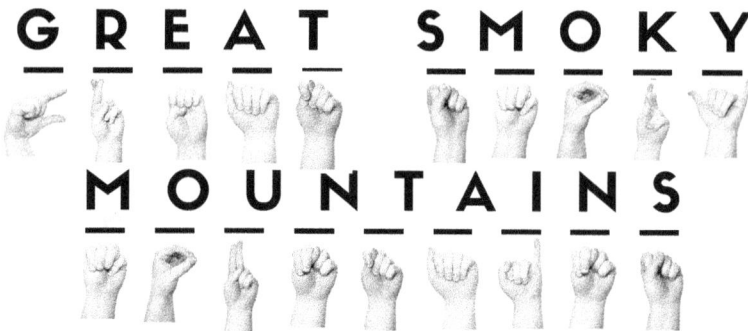

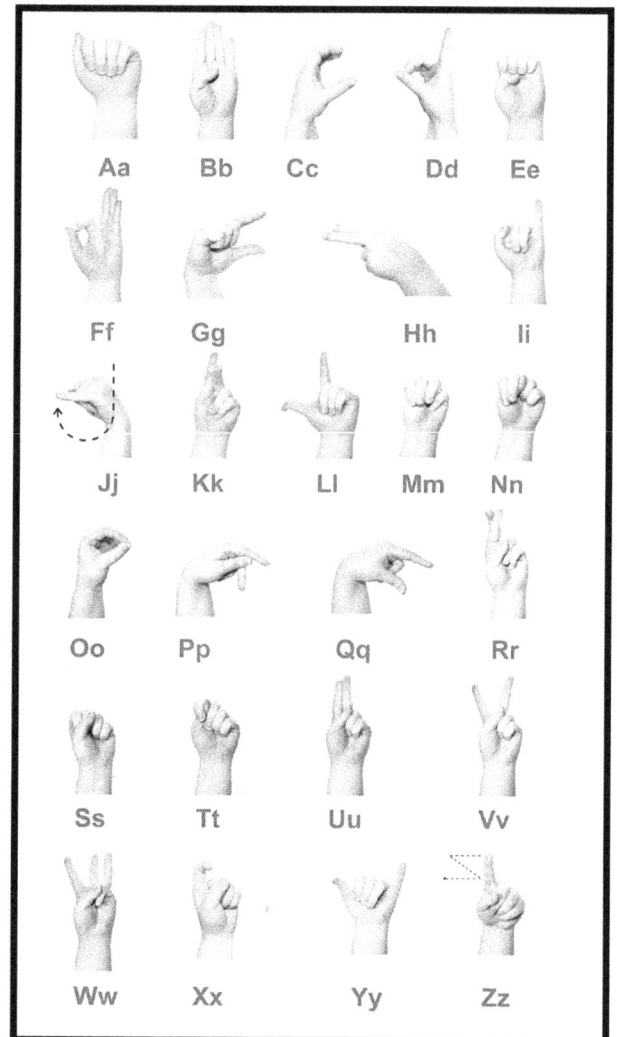

G R E A T S M O K Y

M O U N T A I N S

Aa	Bb	Cc	Dd	Ee
Ff	Gg		Hh	Ii
Jj	Kk	Ll	Mm	Nn
Oo	Pp	Qq		Rr
Ss	Tt	Uu		Vv
Ww	Xx	Yy	Zz	

Hint: Pay close attention to the position of the thumb!

Try it! Using the chart, try to make the letters of the alphabet with your hand. What is the hardest letter to make? Can you spell out your name? Show a friend or family member and have them watch you spell out the name of the national park you are in.

Go Birdwatching at Juniper Ridge Trail

start
here

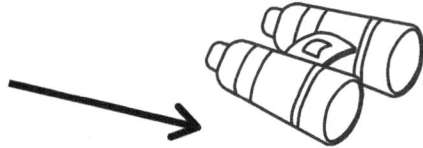

Let's Go Camping
Word Search

1. tent
2. camp stove
3. sleeping bag
4. bug spray
5. sunscreen
6. map
7. flashlight
8. pillow
9. lantern
10. ice
11. snacks
12. smores
13. water
14. first aid kit
15. chair
16. cards
17. books
18. games
19. trail
20. hat

D	P	P	I	L	L	O	W	D	B	T	E	A	C	I
E	O	A	D	P	R	E	A	A	M	B	R	C	A	N
P	W	C	A	M	P	S	T	O	V	E	I	H	X	G
R	A	H	S	G	E	L	E	B	E	E	D	A	P	S
E	L	B	U	G	S	P	R	A	Y	N	G	I	E	A
S	I	A	H	G	C	I	C	N	N	M	E	R	C	N
C	W	N	L	A	F	I	R	S	K	O	O	B	F	K
M	T	A	E	M	I	L	E	L	H	M	R	W	L	J
T	A	P	R	E	A	O	R	E	S	L	B	A	A	B
S	M	P	A	S	R	R	T	E	N	T	L	U	S	C
C	E	A	I	I	R	C	G	P	E	I	U	J	H	A
S	S	N	A	C	K	S	S	I	M	O	K	I	L	R
I	J	R	S	F	O	I	S	N	J	R	A	Q	I	D
C	Y	E	T	L	E	V	E	G	U	O	R	V	G	S
E	W	T	A	K	C	A	B	B	S	S	O	H	H	M
X	J	N	F	I	R	S	T	A	I	D	K	I	T	T
U	A	A	E	S	S	E	N	G	E	T	P	V	A	B
C	J	L	I	A	R	T	D	N	A	M	A	H	A	S

All in the Day of a Park Ranger

There are many right answers for this activity, but not all of the provided examples are good activities for a park ranger. In fact, a park ranger's job may include stopping visitors from doing some of these things.

The list below are activities that rangers do not do:

feed the migratory birds

throw rocks off the side of the mountain

rescue lost hikers

pick wildflowers

share marshmallows with squirrels

catch frogs or toads and make them race

Bats at Carlsbad Caverns

1. CAVE MYOTIS
2. EASTERN RED
3. BIG BROWN
4. HOARY
5. PALLID

Answers: Other National Parks Crossword

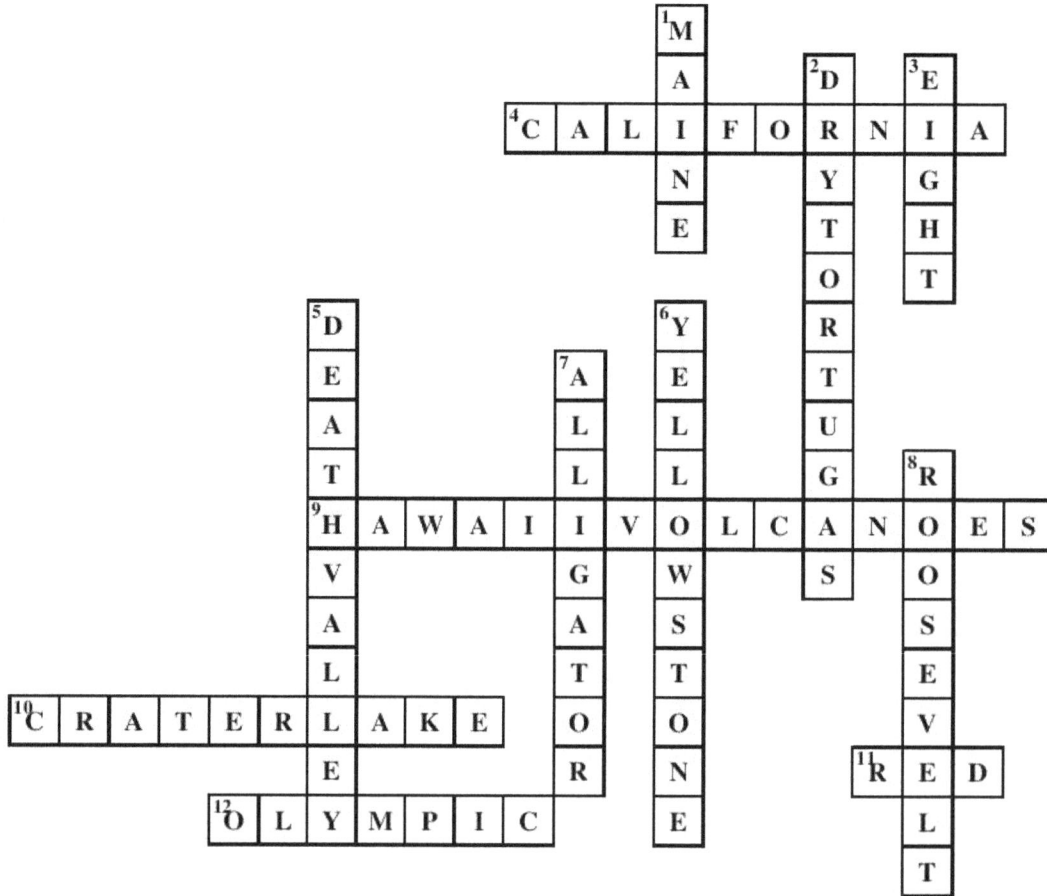

The completed crossword grid reads:

- 4 Across: CALIFORNIA
- 9 Across: HAWAII VOLCANOES
- 10 Across: CRATER LAKE
- 11 Across: RED
- 12 Across: OLYMPIC
- 1 Down: MAINE
- 2 Down: DRY TORTUGAS
- 3 Down: EIGHT
- 5 Down: DEATH VALLEY
- 6 Down: YELLOWSTONE
- 7 Down: ALLIGATOR
- 8 Down: ROOSEVELT

Down

1. State where Acadia National Park is located
2. This National Park has the Spanish word for turtle in it
3. Number of National Parks in Alaska
5. This National Park has some of the hottest temperatures in the world
6. This National Park is the only one in Idaho
7. This toothsome creature can famously be found in Everglades National Park
8. Only president with a national park named for them

Across

4. This state has the most National Parks
9. This park has some of the newest land in the US, caused by a volcanic eruption
10. This park has the deepest lake in the United States
11. This color shows up in the name of a National Park in California
12. This National Park deserves a gold medal

Answers: Which National Park Will You Go To Next?

1. Zion
2. Big Bend
3. Glacier
4. Olympic
5. Sequoia
6. Bryce
7. Mesa Verde
8. Biscayne
9. Wind Cave
10. Great Basin
11. Katmai
12. Yellowstone
13. Voyageurs
14. Arches
15. Badlands
16. Denali
17. Glacier Bay
18. Hot Springs

```
F M M E S A V E R D E B N E Y
E A B I G B E N D E S A S E M
Y L I C A L O Y N E E D L T G
D M G A S S A U C N R L U E R
C E L I I T S C R E O A A K E
S N A W Y E E O I W T N A C A
G I C H A A Q C S E M D N S T
N O I Z P R U T I M R S N E B
I W E L M P O N B W E B K H A
R J R F D N I F L I H B U C S
P A B E E S A N E S O P W R I
S J A E N Y A C S I B A U A N
T C Y I A D O H H Y M E A L R
O T A T L M L E S E G R W R J
H S T O I K A T M A I R O P B
  I C H U R C O L Y M P I C O U
  O Y G T S D E O S B R Y C E T
W I N D C A V E I N R O H E M
```

71

LITTLE BISON
Press

Little Bison Press is an independent children's book publisher based in the Pacific Northwest. We promote exploration, conservation, and adventure through our books. Established in 2021, our passion for outside spaces and travel inspired the creation of Little Bison Press.

We seek to publish books that support children in learning about and caring for the natural places in our world.

To learn more, visit:
www.littlebisonpress.com

Want more free games and activities? Visit our website!